Date in Azar

Shayan Iroomloo Tabrizi

DATE IN AZAR

First edition. May 16, 2024.

Copyright © 2024 Shayan Iroomloo Tabrizi.

ISBN: 979-8224633241

Written by Shayan Iroomloo Tabrizi.

For my mother

SHAYAN IROOMLOO TABRIZI

Preface

Spring, from the past to the present, has always symbolized renewal and freshness in the literature and poetry of the world. But the truth is something else; spring has always only feigned renewal. It feigns love, youth, and beauty. Because it has nothing else to offer. But what is the truth?

Youth is fleeting, leading to maturity, love, and eventually, death. Death, the undeniable truth, the absolute and potential that ultimately becomes actual. This cycle is the unanswered "why" that neither art, nor poetry, nor literature has yet found an answer to. Various theories have been proposed by different sciences regarding this "why," but none have been absolute or unquestionable.

What is Haiku?

Haiku is the shortest poetic form in world literature, originating from Japan and derived from Haikai no renga, a longer Japanese style. This poetic form is not unpopular worldwide, but it has received less attention in Iran. It is said that Hassan Fayyad was one of the first to translate Japanese haikus into Persian, and after him, the late Ahmad Shamlou and Sohrab Sepehri, opened the doors to Japanese haiku for the Iranian reading community.

Although many poets in Iran have written haikus since the 1940s, I still believe that haiku has been overlooked in Iran and is rarely given importance in major literary articles. Haiku is seldom discussed in literary foundations or at conferences.

Now, let's focus on haiku itself. Classical haiku has no complex rules or rhyme. Similarly, its rhythm is not like that of classical Persian or English poetry. These so-called "textual paintings," with their three lines, pull us into their own world—a world that connects with Zen and Japanese paintings, as its origin is "Nihon Koku" or the land of the rising sun. Although it doesn't have complicated rules, this does not mean it follows no rules at all. Classical Japanese haiku consists of seventeen moras (syllables), with five in the first line, seven in the second, and five in the third. Another distinctive feature of Japanese haiku is the prominent presence of "kigo" (seasonal words), which adds color to the poem and conveys emotions through the changing seasons. Additionally, haiku uses "kireji" (cutting words) at the end of one of the three sections of the poem, which contributes to the rhythm and musicality of the verse.

But My Haiku...

My haikus have gone through many struggles to be seen. They carry a romantic, melancholic, and sometimes dark essence. Sometimes they are classical, following the strict rules of Japanese poetry, while other times, they are modern, breaking those rules. But the one constant in all of them is loneliness, the same loneliness that has been humanity's companion from birth to death.

In the end, this book is not just the result of a year of my mental paintings, merely a few lines for the reader's imagination. Rather, it is the relentless efforts of a writer who has spent several years trying to publish his dreams and transfer them to the literary world. I am grateful to my dear brothers, Arvin Zarei and Alireza Goshtaei, as well as to all the friends who have assisted me along the way. And finally, I thank myself, for always believing in myself throughout this journey.

Shayan Iroomloo Tabrizi

1

The pelicans have migrated to their nests
from the winter,
and I, to the winter

2

The mirror was mad—
it showed me to myself,
but I longed for you.

3

I want to hold you in my arms for hours.
And perhaps,
only the hours know this.

4

I am winter—
Cold, lifeless, empty of gazes.
Without you

5

Our tea went cold again—
So much that, in your absence,
I stared at the empty wall.

6

Come, let's play again.
I'll count with my eyes closed.
But for the love of God, this time— let me find you.

7

Without you
every night is
Yalda[1]

1. Yalda night, the longest night of the year, marks the last night of autumn. This ancient festival, celebrated by many around the world, has long been an important tradition for Iranians.

8

You are Yalda,
everything after you
is merely the winter morning.

9

I wrote
I wrote
I wrote; erased

10

Time stands still in the cafes we were together,
My coffee grows cold,
And I, drink our memories.

11

Your eyes are a ghazal[1] by Hafez,
And I, the mute man
That Hafez recites.

1. A form of Persian poetry typically associated with themes of love, mysticism, and wisdom. Hafez, a prominent Iranian poet, wrote ghazals that are considered a vital part of Iranian culture and literature

12

The yellow leaves
gave way to dry stems.
Your footprints to snows

13

Call my name,
In this city, only
You know how I'll return

14

This city has dissolved you into itself.
You are nowhere,
but I see you everywhere.

15

Loneliness is a mountain that is distant.
With the desert, with the sea, with the forest,
Even, with itself.

16

My days pass like this,
Half of it in memory of you,
And the other half, remembering you.

17

How lonely!
in your absence
I died every night until morning

18

Every day I recite ten Tasbīḥ[1]
Oh God, let me forget her...
No, God forbid

1. Tasbīḥ is a tool used in Islamic prayer and dhikr (remembrance of God), often consisting of a string of beads to aid in reciting praises of God.

19

Let's part ways,
You come toward me,
I'll run toward you

20

It will end,
The pain that every day,
Cries me out in the void

21

Silence!
The only music I listen to under the moonlight,
With the branches, reminding me of you

22

And it is only your shadow,
that remains
after the desert storm of my heart.

23

Sometimes I say to myself:
Perhaps I am dead,
for I no longer see you.

24

This last separation will kill me.

Look at the sunflower fields.

From spring to summer, they become prisoners of the downpour

25

You are my motherland.
I have emigrated from you,
But I will never forget you.

26

You will gather your longing in a suitcase,
From the meadow path, you will head toward me,
And you will cry hard on the way to the cemetery.

27

You found your excuse
to leave.
I, for dying.

28

"I will feel better.
I'm fine, oh..."
Again, he wiped her face

29

We were all turned to ash,
but a single particle of us
still burns.

30

Do you look at our photos?
The ones that still drive me crazy,
The stress of seeing the photo of your eyes!

31

I must
experience death,
This time, it will truly end.

32

She still speaks at night.
The gypsy girl, under the moonlight,
with me, in me.

33

We are pregnant with history.
bury us alive,
with history, in history.

34

Our crows
count the days
for your return.

35

You came with persimmons

You left in the Golabgiri[1]
Come back with the figs.

1. Golabgiri is a ceremony held in the months of Ordibehesht and Khordad in the cities of Ghamsar, Kashan, and Isfahan (Iran). This tradition involves the distillation of roses to extract rosewater.

36

How many doors in front of me
After you
Became a wall

37

The grapevines of the yard,
After you,
Only bear wine.

38

I am the desert,
And you are the spring cloud,
Rain down on my dry and black body.

39

What a place you've given me refuge,
Behind the memories of winter,
Under the rubble.

40

She has braided her hair,
Runs her fingers through its curls,
Under the cold rain, the gypsy girl.

41

We reached the waves,
The waves brought the news,
The ocean drowned all the memories.

42

In the end, this darkness will fade.
I will find the light,
If there is a sun.

43

I went to our usual café,
Ordered two coffees,
I forgot you had left.

44

The calendar shows 365 days,
But the mirror reflects 365 years
Without you.

45

I have forgotten
The nights without you
When I used to think of your presence.

46

Years must pass
For me to forget
That I have not forgotten you.

47

You are like my shadow under the moonlight,
I come running,
You run away.

48

I remember,
I choke, I laugh,
And again, I choke.

49

Every night on the wall of my room,
The shadow of a lonely man smokes a cigarette,
And then, quietly, he dies.

50

I love this city, crowded as it is,
Maybe I'll see someone for a moment,
Who resembles you.

51

Suddenly, it becomes winter
In a hot summer
When I think of you.

52

The cold of winter promises the buds of spring
The buds promise the flowers of summer
And the flowers, separation and sorrow.

53

I don't understand politics
Every four years
I vote for your return.

54

They said: "You don't need your national ID to vote"
I hope one day they will say
To see you, no waiting is needed anymore.

55

The darkness has covered the sky
Morning will not come
Unless you open your eyes.

56

Did you know, under the rubble of your gaze, I die
You just looked at me
Then, you didn't even look at me anymore.

57

I am the emptiest parking lot
In the busiest neighborhood
Empty capacity: one

58

This is not fair at all
Does man have one more life?
So why do I die every night?

59

I blow through the window, without a shadow
I smell your hair, and leave
You are still lying on the bed like a flower

60

Among your hair, a poem should be made
Crawling and reaching the legends
Kissed, reaching the end

61

Between us is a distance like the sea
A distance that can be filled
Like my shirt, with your body

62

Each one ties a DAK̲ĪL[1] something on this journey
This poor, godless soul
Has tied his DAK̲ĪL to the wave of your straight hair

1. DAK̲ĪL "interceder," a piece of rag or cord or a lock fastened (dak̲īl bast
an) on a sacred place or object, for example, the railing around a saint's tomb or grave
or a public fountain (saqqā-k̲āna), the branch of a tree considered sacred, or another
plant (e.g., Šahrī, V, p. 113, VI, p. 10; Šakūrzāda, pp. 91-92; cf. Dehk̲odā, s.v.), to
obtain a desired benefit.

63

The eyes are waiting,
The hands are pleading,
And in this way, borders kill the human.

64

"Looks like you'll be late"
He says this and kisses the photo
And flies from the roof.

65

From in front of my gaze to the farthest station,
You pass, you pass, you pass,
And I, only, gaze.

66

Then it sets,
What lies within me,
And rises, what is not within you.

67

It breaks
The silence of the white room,
With its bloody coughs.

68

Your eyes
Your gaze
... My heart

69

Her lips were red
Even when
She didn't eat wild raspberries.

70

A lone pregnant woman,
Under the spring rain,
Watches the young lovers

71

Wind and blizzard,
Rain, rain, rain,
Flood—oh—sigh.

72

I drown,
In the wild depth of your gaze,
Instantly.

73

"Who knows when it will end?"
He whispered this
And gently laid his head on the ground.

74

She sits beside me, a fallen woman,
Slowly savoring her Nescafé,
Then leaves.

75

You forgave yourself because you loved him.
I forgave you because I loved you.
Full stop.

76

I became silence
So I could sing
Songs for you.

77

We died many times,
And yet,
We are still alive.

78

Every night,
Homeless soldiers
Commit suicide in my head.

79

I am from winter, you, the autumn alley.
Damn that day of
Cherry blossoms.

80

"For the last time, I ask,
Do you love me?"
And kisses the photo.

81

The right corner of my lips
Still tastes like pomegranate,
The one we didn't eat on Yalda.

82

What do these couples want?
From the sleepless body
Of Tehran's streets.

83

Seagulls chase their prey,
And the fish wait for the hunter.
Both dance.

84

Now I stand at a distance,
Under the rain still,
Watching you is sweet.

85

The blue-eyed snake
no longer sheds its skin,
The one that fell in love years ago

86

For years, I have walked this wheat road,
Every day, on foot, toward the unknown.
A little in your place, a little in mine.

87

Autumn, they smoke under the rain
Winter is frozen
But, if you were mine...

88

Everything ends,
Like the song you used to sing to me,
Only its scars remain on my desert-like body.

89

Look well,
Find a madman under the rain
Who still loves you.

90

The wind dances on your hair
Your eyes behind the glasses
Always smile without your lips.

91

You leave, every day
From the last path
Of the blizzard in my heart.

92

In my heart, it is bright
You will return
The sun of Winter.

93

Which one rains more,
An autumn cloud
Or a puppy that has been abandoned?

94

My days after you
Are autumn dreams,
But it's winter.

95

In panic!
A sunflower in winter
Searches for the sun behind the clouds.

96

Baby sparrow
Spring
Hail

97

In your slaughterhouse, I became flesh
Sit down,
Listen to my heart.

98

Our date is green[1]
late autumn
Around Shiraz

1. "Our date is green" refers to a concept in Persian where "green" symbolizes something being in place, fresh, or in harmony, often used in the context of a plan or agreement.

About the Author

Shayan Iroomloo Tabrizi is an Iranian writer, poet, film critic, researcher, and artist born on January 23, 1996, in Tehran. He holds a bachelor's degree in microbiology and a master's degree in dramatic literature. Over the past decade, he has written numerous stories, screenplays, and plays, alongside serving as the editor of an academic arts magazine.

His artistic achievements include publishing several books in Iran and Canada, directing a short film, and acting in theatre, films, and TV series. As a film critic, he has written analytical reviews on Iranian and world cinema, focusing on themes, cinematic techniques, and narrative structures. His critiques have been published on his personal website as well as in a Persian magazine in Vancouver.

Beyond writing and cinema, he is also a passionate photographer, specializing in street photography. His works have been recognized in competitions in Vancouver, and he has won awards for his compelling visual storytelling.

Currently residing in Vancouver, British Columbia, he continues to explore storytelling through literature, cinema, and photography, seeking to capture emotions and narratives that transcend time and space.

Read more at https://shayaniroomlootabriz.com/.